SYMBOLS OF AMERICAN FREEDOM

The United States Flag

by Kirsten Chang

BELLWETHER MEDIA • MINNEAPOLIS, MN

Note to Librarians, Teachers, and Parents:

Blastoff! Readers are carefully developed by literacy experts and combine standards-based content with developmentally appropriate text.

Level 1 provides the most support through repetition of high-frequency words, light text, predictable sentence patterns, and strong visual support.

Level 2 offers early readers a bit more challenge through varied simple sentences, increased text load, and less repetition of high-frequency words.

Level 3 advances early-fluent readers toward fluency through increased text and concept load, less reliance on visuals, longer sentences, and more literary language.

Level 4 builds reading stamina by providing more text per page, increased use of punctuation, greater variation in sentence patterns, and increasingly challenging vocabulary.

Level 5 encourages children to move from "learning to read" to "reading to learn" by providing even more text, varied writing styles, and less familiar topics.

Whichever book is right for your reader, Blastoff! Readers are the perfect books to build confidence and encourage a love of reading that will last a lifetime!

This edition first published in 2019 by Bellwether Media, Inc.

No part of this publication may be reproduced in whole or in part without written permission of the publisher. For information regarding permission, write to Bellwether Media, Inc., Attention: Permissions Department, 6012 Blue Circle Drive, Minnetonka, MN 55343.

Library of Congress Cataloging-in-Publication Data

LC record for The United States Flag available at https://lccn.loc.gov/2017061632

Text copyright © 2019 by Bellwether Media, Inc. BLASTOFF! READERS and associated logos are trademarks and/or registered trademarks of Bellwether Media, Inc. SCHOLASTIC, CHILDREN'S PRESS, and associated logos are trademarks and/or registered trademarks of Scholastic Inc., 557 Broadway, New York, NY 10012.

Editor: Rebecca Sabelko   Designer: Andrea Schneider

Printed in the United States of America, North Mankato, MN.

Table of Contents

What Is the United States Flag?

The United States flag is a **symbol** for **freedom** and **unity**.

The flag is red, white, and blue. It has 13 stripes and 50 stars.

The stripes are for the first 13 **colonies**. The stars are for the 50 states.

Flag History

The first flag was made in 1776. It had 13 stars and stripes.

Betsy Ross,
first flag maker

The flag meant the U.S. was free from British rule.

The country grew. With each new state, a star was added to the flag.

Names for the U.S. Flag:

- The Stars and Stripes
- The Star-Spangled Banner
- Old Glory
- The Red, White, and Blue

Fly the Flag

The flag flies at schools, **libraries**, and government buildings.

June 14 is Flag Day.
Americans fly the
flag proudly.

19

Americans **respect**
the U.S. flag.
They fly it high!

Glossary

colonies

areas controlled by another country

respect

to admire or honor

freedom

the state of being free

symbol

something that stands for something else

libraries

places where people use or borrow books and other materials

unity

when a group of people agree

To Learn More

AT THE LIBRARY

Brannon, Cecelia H. *Zoom in on the US Flag*. New York, N.Y.: Enslow Publishing, 2017.

Chang, Kirsten. *The Pledge of Allegiance*. Minneapolis, Minn.: Bellwether Media, 2019.

Clay, Kathryn. *The U.S. Flag: Introducing Primary Sources*. North Mankato, Minn.: Capstone Press, 2016.

ON THE WEB

Learning more about the United States flag is as easy as 1, 2, 3.

1. Go to www.factsurfer.com.

2. Enter "United States flag" into the search box.

3. Click the "Surf" button and you will see a list of related web sites.

With factsurfer.com, finding more information is just a click away.

Index

The images in this book are reproduced through the courtesy of: Kit Leong, front cover; Leonard Zhukovsky, p. 3; Joe Guetzloff, pp. 4-5; Donald R. Swartz, pp. 6-7; Monkey Business Images, pp. 8-9, 22 (middle right); H.A. Thomas & Charles Wylie & Weisgerber/ Alamy, pp. 10-11; TFoxFoto, pp. 14-15; carterdayne pp. 16-17; Mila May, pp. 18-19; Scott Cornell, pp. 20-21; fstop123, p. 22 (middle left); Ricardo Reitmeyer, p. 22 (top right); Pressmaster, p. 22 (bottom left); Monthira, p. 22 (bottom right).